ALL THE SHADES OF THE HEART

POETRY OF LOVE AND LIFE

SERAPH

Made with ♥ on the Notion Press Platform
www.notionpress.com

For all my dreams, lost and fulfilled.

Contents

Contents

Preface

From cringeworth teenage songs, to poetry in my young adulthood, here is a collection of poems written about love, dreams, life and fantasies from a hopeless fantasy loving romantic. I've published this book anonymously because I've articulated my deepest and darkest feelings. Hopefully there are more books to come!

I hope you enjoy it!

1. A Higher Existence

Be the wind at night... that blows through their soul,
and sends chills down your spine,
Be the flowers of exotic jungles,
intoxicate with your sight and smell.
Be the smell of the earth after rain,
sweet nostalgia.
Be the soul they always wanted to bare open,
naked and untamed.
Be the stars of the night sky,
a far away dream they try to reach.

2. Release

Butterflies in the sky,
Make my heart fly.
I blow my spirit from my hand,
I know who I am.
I release,
Spirit at ease.
Let all the darkness leave,
The hell hounds heave.

3. Drifting

Caught in stasis between heaven and hell;
Stuck on this earth, inside my shell.
Memories seem vague, what's fake and what's real,
I hope you know the way I feel.
My spirit is chained, my dreams run loose;
My body is mine, but knows only abuse.
I can't be your star ,but I could fill my void
With all the pain you hold inside.
You feel like home, soft and warm,
I just want to hold you in my arms.

4. Shadow

My dark side is gentle.
My shadow was created to protect me,
I can be bright because he channels my darkness.
He tells me it's okay to be sad.
His spirit is with me, he is me.
He makes me stronger,
Reminding me to bare my fangs
When they step too close.

5. Longing

Ever since I saw you
I wondered how it could be,
If Through my eyes you could see
How You make my dried garden of a life green.
I say your name through lips parched
As through consciousness in and out I march.
A sparkling fairy in midst of this terrible world
You made my thoughts stand when frantically they had swirled.
The first and last time you held me in your arms
It washed away the nightmares pain and harm.
I remember your inner child's dreams as I remember my own,
And My heart never wishes for you to be alone.
Exhilarating as Rain upon this desert sand
But Broken as bones
Here I am.
Skin upon skin you excite me so bare
For you I would shed my fears and despair.
My eyes fill with tears and and even god seems real,
When I remember how he created you dear.

6. Rush

You are a streak of rainbow in my monochrome life,
and the rush of adrenaline before the fall
and I spread my wings.
How can you be so afraid of something
and yet be so desperate for it?
Catch me. Dont catch me.
Let me feel the rush even so.
You bring that sparkle to my eye,
that spring to my step,
and set my mind afire
with dreams and songs.
Keep me forever by your side.
You are every happy memory flashing before my eyes,
so is this the beginning or the end?

7. Matrix

You spark my circuits when we touch.

We're on the same network,

your Protocols synchronize with my soul.

Glitch, Glitch, Glitch my existence.

I was working perfectly fine before,

now a 404 error when i try to process my thoughts.

Run just my trial version,

or pay with your heart.

Detached from my hardware,

you can't reach me from there.

Run the right program,

to decipher my software and reach inside,

deeper than anyone has gone.

8. Intertwine

Brush your lips against my face.
Go down and speak to me,
I want to feel your deep voice
reverberate against my neck
Trace your fingers down my spine
as our ancient souls intertwine,
in a dance that was meant to be.
Can you bring tears to my eyes
with that pleasure?
Show me, how deep your soul is then.

9. Let go

Hurt me like you always do.
Break me, a broken soul.
It takes a special kind of person to do that.
I feel myself letting go.
When the anger fades,
and there is nothing left,
I wonder.. do I love you,
or hate myself?
Slowly my being,
my DNA ..unravelling,
My soul is a gentle mist from my mouth
with every breath I let out.
Sweet melancholy peace
is all that i feel,
as I see the world through blurry eyes,
Becoming one with the black velvet sky.

10. Love is a Flame

Love is a flame they say, don't hold on to it.

It will burn you they say, don't have hope in it, it is fickle and fragile.

So do you turn to stone for warmth?

Do you look to the cold moon, hoping that your trees will grow?

You search for warmth in safe places, damp and cold, beneath the Earth where it is familiar to you.

Everything is hollow, fake and comforting, the walls echo what you want to hear.

Come above your den, touch this flame, and learn for the first time.. What it is like to truly feel and be alive.

Whether it is gentle and warm.. or harsh and scorching.. Feel.

Wake up from your eternal dream.

Wake up and feel.

11. Underground

You woke me up from my deep slumber
Ripping my roots from underground,
Wiping the dust from my face.
We bleed the same i see,
But will I make it better?
Dont come back with me into the Earth.
Somehow.. someway take me far from this birth.

12. Lazy Summer Afternoon

You make me want to curl up in warm sunshine,
soaking in the sunlight streaming between green leaves,
Dreaming of sweet, sweet nostalgia.
Oh how you make even bitter memories seem sweet,
And how you make just everything better Darling.

13. The Search

Show me Vanilla Skies and chocolate rain,

But I'd rather walk this path of pain,

They only saw roses but I felt the thorns,

Yes I'm awfully sick, sick with love.

What was alive in my heart was almost dead and gone.

True Love demands a sacrifice, I feel like I've been paying all my life.

Roses are red and Violets are blue,

All my life my soul was searching for you.

I looked deep within my soul seeking the answers for my aching heart,

I hope to the Lord that for any longer we are not apart.

14. Soothe me

Gentle rain,
Your love upon my pain,
You send gentle rain,
From heaven again and again.
Soothe my soul,
Through which restlessness bores,
Like the moon, many craters on my heart,
But you fill with love whole.
In the darkest of nights,
I seek your face,
When nights seem endless
And the Earth a barren place.
In the day when sun rises,
My soul still awaits,
Your return my King!
My soul renewed again.

15. Air and Water

Like Air and Water,

We spiral around eachother,

a storm.

From the moment we met,

we knew something beautiful was born.

Our minds spark as they touch,

our bodies tremble as our hands brush,

is this something forever, or just a passing rush?

Our souls empty out onto eachother,

dissapearing like water into sand,

sinking deep into the Earth.

Could this be fated, meant to be from birth?

As we look into the sky, at the moon and stars,

we realize together how small we are,

no matter how different we are in every way,

none of it matters if we are willing to stay.

I will hold your hand in your darkest hours,

Wipe every my tear, and before no fear I'll cower,

Back to back against the world,

that's what it means to be your girl.

16. Comet's Ride

Take me on a comet's ride,
To far away galaxies and stars,
You took me out of this pit I threw myself into,
All without even realizing it.
Who knows on this journey of life,
Where it may end or where we may go,
Insignificant these feelings may seem to you now,
But it takes time for the most magnificent trees to grow.
Every kind word you say,
Gives me the strength to go on another day,
Though I may never say it to you,
But maybe someday this poem may be due.
I am not a simple person, though simple I may seem,
I hide myself well, behind a mask that has thickened for years,
Far from perfect, my demons take over at times,
But I try to be brave, fighting them day after day, night after night.
You touched my life in a beautiful way,
And maybe you might be one to stay,
What better way to mend broken souls,
Than to put the two together, and make both whole?

17. Kindred spirit

I just met you,
Drunk and high,
Why do I see so much of my life in another's eyes?
Maybe I've fallen. Fallen in love
Heal me. Heal me all in all.
Fall. Fall. Fall.
What is life?
Just coincidences.. meeting beautiful souls.
All with different thoughts and goals.
But take care.. stay alive.
For me.. for the people you will meet, darling.
Hope is all I eat, it's all I dream.
It's all I stay alive on , silly as it may seem.
Young and naive.
Take care darling.
The world is cruel,
But I know you have already seen it all.
Seen so many things, you should not have.
Was it my fault.. was it God's?
All I can do is hold you.

18. Butterflies

If we were little butterflies, making love between the flowers
Would I be happier.. would my wings be lighter,
Not having to carry the weight of an entire lifetime?
Sipping sweet honey, flitting between the petals of our youth,
We would love with an intoxication, without fear of
consequence or reason..
The way love is meant to be.

19. Monochrome

Day after day...I think of you next to me,
In every moment you used to be,
That streak of color... that vein of life
I held on to when I couldnt see through the pain.
Now you became that pain,
Blurring my eyes so I cant see,
Now I cant care, nothing is clear anymore.
Nothing is real anymore.
How I wish you were here,
I saw my soul in your eyes,
I would give anything to hear your cries,
So I could come running back to hold you.
Everything is one color,
why does no one seem close to me,
Everyone is so far,
Tell me... where you are.

20. Gentle

Just a gentle touch, maybe just maybe,
do I dare to hope, dream or pray ,
That you could be the one.
Too scared,too fragile, too scarred,
Brittle like glass, hard like diamond.
We touch eachother gently.. longingly,
Searching eachothers eyes so deeply,
Eachothers souls .. for something that was lost to us a long
time ago,
Hold me in your arms
That is all I will ever ask of you.
Hold me and tell me.. everything will be alright.

21. The Ordinary

As ordinarily as the earth turns,
As it's molten core ever burns,
So my love for you ever churns,
Like the oceans and the seas.
Deep beneath my stoic mask
My tired soul longs to be with you at last.
You seem to be the oasis far out of reach
A mirage from the gods, they test my hunger and greed.
Yes you are like a pot of gold for the miser
The last food for a criminal on his knees,
The sunset on my days of sin,
My beautiful celestial soul mate and twin.

22. You will never know

As the seasons turn,
And day becomes night,
I think of you ,
You are my light .
The leaves they change ,
They fall to the ground
But as my tears fall down they make no sound.
Alone and loneliness , me myself and I,
I remember when I first saw you as an innocent child.
I would take that chance , take that leap,
But for all that bravery you're too precious to me.
You'll never know how I said your name,
As I lost my mind , the universe it claimed.
You'll never know how I speak of you,
Your sweet soul and gentle mind,
I wonder in me what you might find.

23. Want

My wordless cries,
My wordless cries for help.
I cry for you,
I cry for you so loud in my head.
I think of you,
I think of you so hard.
I dream of you,
I dream of you so hungry.
I pray for you,
Pray for you, the most sinful nun on her knees,
I would do anything you please.
I could think of a thousand ways to say I love you,
But have no idea when and where to say it ,
Not a clue, and I have not the grit .
I could think of a hundred ways to make you happy,
But I have not the courage , it makes me so angry.

24. A Photo

There you are so sterile and sweet,
A mind and smile to bring me to my knees.
I gaze at your photo just for a rush,
That's all it takes, my heart is gushed.
All the venom the world has put into my veins,
It melts away when I see your face.
King of my heart,
Forever and ever in me you will reign.
My fairy tale prince and knight in shining armour,
To be your princess would be the greatest of honours.

25. The Man

Sweetest of boys , yet a tad bit sultry,
Bored with people, all the while busy.
He prefers dark academia but light fantasy.
His eyes are so deep and so open is his heart.
Sassy at times but more than anyone is smart.
He keeps his voice soft , but likes his whiskey hard.

26. So Far

My future seems far , so far away.
I take each tomorrow, day by day.
But a future with you is what I hope,
It's what I dreamed since long ago.
As a child you were my perfection incarnate
My forbidden fruit, my precious star,
And now like my future you seem so far.

27. Your Name

Soft as feathers and as sweet as rain,
That's how I feel when I say your name.
I love the feeling in my mouth,
The way my tongue twists and turns about.
I wish it was magic and I could have you here,
Just say one word,
And have you appear!

28. One Too Many

I had one too many drinks,
You held me , you didn't even think.
I felt like a goddess drunk,
And you were my pious monk.
Night time Neon lights were blurred,
To others my heart is stone, but for you it purred.
Oh I knew only your arms, I forgot all harm.
Sweet as honey, and smooth as ice,
You're my cherry pie , my greatest vice.

29. Every time

• 29 •

Every time you feel alone,
I wish you would think of me.
Every time you feel far,
Please think of each beautiful star, each far apart.
Every time you cry please know,
I'd never let one tear fall to the floor.
Every time you feel depressed,
Know your demons are mine , just suppressed.
Every time you look at the moon,
Know we are under the same one,
My sweet lotus, bloom.

30. Scarred

You are a flame in my dark, oh I yearn,
My soul , I can't lie, for you it burns.
I am a moth to your light,
Won't you turn and see my plight.
Afraid to get too close I might get singed,
Afraid to get too far , this dark mind unhinged.
You like the sun, and I the Earth , surfaces scarred,
I wish i could just revolve around you like a constant star.

31. Desire

• 31 •

As the seas crash into rock,
I want to crash into you.
As Two planets collide,
Inhibitions aside.
As the Elements entwine
I want you to be mine.
I want to arch my back
As all fades into utter black.
Through every lifetime,
As universe fades into night,
The two of us join in the dance divine.

32. Pain

Angels come lift me,
To the sky , I want to die.
Demons turn my face ,
From my lips drip tears
And my eyes seem crazed,
love is the cause for ,
All my fears .
Someone hold me down,
Impossible is making this mouth,
smile from frown.
Gods come and bury me underground,
Take me from this place where I'm bound.

33. Love's Fool

Won't you look at me love,
You're all I asked for
From those angels above.
Look at me and smile,
I want to feel this ice heart melt,
For a while.
You're all my heart dreams of
I would worship you,
If I had not worldly scruples.
I wish we were one and not a lonely two.
My heart is locked in a deadly duel,
i'm love's prisoner and I'm love's fool,
will I dream for me or dream of you.

34. Above and Beneath

• 34 •

Delicate that I am,

I crumble into you,

When you hold me in your arms

My tears fall on cue.

Be gentle with me I say,

It's only you I crave.

To have your fingers down my spine

I shiver,

Anticipating your lips mine quiver.

To hear you say my name

Sends a warmth from my feet.

I'd live for you and die for you,

For all above hell and heaven beneath.

35. Incarnate

Drifting through a cosmic stream,
I think I saw you in a dream.
Through the ripples of time and space
I try to reach out and touch your face,
Alas it was just a test,
The universe will never let me rest.
I reincarnate against the will,
Of all the gods , oh but still,
In vain I try to find you so,
Through mystic deeps, trouble and woe.

36. This Mask

Can I be loved I ask.
I've been hurt so much,
I wear this mask.
Can you see the real me,
Is it dream or reality?
I thought when I was young
I was brave and tough,
But years gone by,
Have turned me rough.
I wish to shed this thick skin off me,
Oh once again to feel young and free,
And to feel happiness and hope
And to love you selflessly so.

37. Twilight Sky

My heart is the colour of the twilight sky,
Fading away into the dusk,
My body is weak and soul a husk,
Compared to what I used to be,
In the mirror I can't even recognise me.
But you are brilliant and beautiful as old,
All the colours of the cotton candy starry fold.
You've never changed and you never will,
You've retained your youthful charms and boyish thrill.
I've always looked up to you,
And treasured your very name.
Damn them who don't value you
But they would never know this pain.

38. In My Veins

Inject your venom into my veins,
I want to feel this high
And feel this pain.
I'll be your addict till I overdose,
Just to see a glimpse of heaven,
I can suffer death's throes.
These blinding highs and seething lows
When you ignore me it's like the greatest of blows.
It's like a brand on my skin and cut on my tongue,
I'll live another day when you tell me love ,
that I'm the one.

39. Stay

Stay with me.
I am quiet,
be still if you want to hear my voice.
I am gentle, like the swaying of the branches in the breeze,
No, I would never force you,
never hold you,
except to keep you warm and safe,
my tears fall softly,
never heard, never seen.
Stay,
A soft cry in the dark.

40. Not your Face

I had not seen your face,
But I knew your heart.
Do you admire me as you would, a work of art?
Beautiful you said, not knowing what it meant,
To me, a discarded rose broken and bent.
Star-crossed lovers.. our paths have met,
Destiny has doomed us, peace brief and yet,
only compels these kisses to be ever more desperate.